W9-BFS-906

FORTS OF THE WEST

This star-shaped fort on the Gulf of Mexico is typical of many of the military encampments established in the west during the second half of the 19th century.

FORTS OF THE WEST

BETHANNE KELLY PATRICK

MASON CREST PUBLISHERS

Mason Crest Publishers
370 Reed Road
Broomall PA 19008
www.masoncrest.com

First printing

1 3 5 7 9 8 6 4 2

Library of Congress Cataloging-in-Publication Data
on file at the Library of Congress

ISBN 1-59084-071-2

Publisher's note: many of the quotations in this book come from
original sources, and contain the spelling and grammatical
inconsistencies of the original text.

CONTENTS

1 ENCAMPMENT:
FORT CLATSOP, OREGON   6

2 COLONIZATION:
THE PRESIDIO OF
SAN FRANCISCO   14

3 ENCAMPMENT:
FORT LEAVENWORTH,
KANSAS   22

4 EXPANSION:
FORT LARAMIE, WYOMING   30

5 EXPULSION:
FORT SILL, OKLAHOMA   38

6 MODERNIZATION:
FORT HOOD, TEXAS   48

GLOSSARY   56

TIMELINE   58

FURTHER READING   60

INTERNET RESOURCES   61

INDEX   62

👆 This reconstruction of Fort Clatsop, Lewis and Clark's winter camp in1805, was built near Astoria, Oregon. Fort Clatsop was the first American fort built at the western edge of the frontier.

ENCAMPMENT: FORT CLATSOP, OREGON

their own civilization. Yet their first sight of the Pacific Ocean
in November 1805 thrilled them: "Great joy in camp. We are in
view of the ocean…which we have been so long anxious to
see, and the roaring or noise made by the waves breaking on
the rocky shores (as I suppose) may be heard distinctly."

Captain William Rogers Clark wrote those words on
November 7, 1805. He, Captain Meriwether Lewis, and their
Corps of Discovery had just trekked through the new
Louisiana Purchase, across the Continental Divide, and to their
nation's westernmost limits. Their orders from President
Thomas Jefferson had been to explore the Missouri River to
its source, to establish the most direct land route to the
Pacific, and to make scientific and geographic observations
along the way.

While Lewis and Clark had reached their goal in the late
fall of 1805, their journey was not over. Winter would soon

Not every member of the Corps of Discovery was human. Captain Meriwether Lewis brought along his dog, "Seaman," who survived the trip.

come to the Pacific Northwest. The Corps of Discovery could not turn around and head home. They would have to camp where they were, in Oregon.

They needed shelter first. On December 7, the captains chose a "place of encampment" at a high point near a creek, where they believed there would be plenty of game to hunt. On that spot they built a timber fort that members of the Corps of Discovery would call home until March 23, 1806.

The Corps of Discovery was a military expedition, and most of its members were soldiers in the U.S. Army. Georges Drouillard, the group's most skilled hunter, supplied the camp with elk meat, which was high in protein but also tough and bland. Lewis had chosen to camp near the coast because he and his men craved salt after months of eating primitive food.

Built close to a natural spring, Fort Clatsop was 50 feet square. It had two long structures connected front and back by gates. On either side of a parade ground were entrances to the longhouses. One of those served as the enlisted men's quarters and the other held the captains' quarters; a room for Toussaint le Charbonneau, his Native American wife Sacagawea, and their infant son; the orderly room; and a **smokehouse**.

The soldiers' quarters at Fort Clatsop were simple, but served their purpose for the people who were stationed there. Everyday life at the fort could be either boring or difficult.

The smokehouse was probably the most important room to the group at Fort Clatsop. They were often hungry. At this stage in their travels, meals consisted of spoiled fish and a few roots. On Christmas Day 1805 Clark wrote that dinner "concisted of pore Elk, So much Spoiled that we eate it thro' mear necessity," and on New Year's Day 1806 the explorers toasted "with our only bevereage *pure water*," wrote Lewis.

During the weeks at Fort Clatsop, commanding officers Lewis and Clark would be busy updating their journals and

Sacagawea was a great help to the success of the Lewis and Clark expedition. She kept the Corps of Discovery safe numerous times by translating their peaceful intentions to suspicious Native Americans. To the Indians that Lewis and Clark met, the fact that they had a woman with their group meant that the expedition was not a war party.

checking the data they had gathered on plants, animals, and Native American tribes. They also had to correct and check their maps, an especially important job because the two leaders had decided to return by a different and more efficient route.

However, the enlisted men at Fort Clatsop did not have much to do. Clark realized that if the soldiers were left idle and anxious, he and Lewis would soon have all manner of trouble. So he organized a salt-extraction camp down the coast. Five large kettles were used to boil seawater until it evaporated and left pure salt. When the salt-making soldiers brought samples to Fort Clatsop in early January 1806, Lewis pronounced their product "excellent, fine, strong, & white…This was a great treat to myself and most of the party." With salt, the Fort Clatsop diet of boiled, dried, "jerked," and fresh elk could be varied a little.

While Fort Clatsop was named after a local Indian tribe, Lewis and Clark named many other places they discovered after friends, family members, and famous people. For example, a small river near the Rocky Mountains was named "Judith's Creek" after a cousin of Meriwether Lewis.

Unfortunately, Lewis and Clark could do little to improve the rest of camp life. The Northwest weather consisted of rain, damp fog, and more rain—it rained every day but 12 out of the 106 days the Corps of Discovery stayed at Fort Clatsop. The dampness rotted clothes, attracted insects, and gave most of the men colds and other illnesses.

Visiting Native Americans provided some variety to the daily routine. Clark described the Indians as "close bargainers." Their trading for items such as otter skins, seal meat, fish, roots, elk meat, and canoes quickly depleted the "gift" supplies the explorers had brought with them. Lewis and Clark wrote often in their journals about the Native American tribes, their appearance, habits, living conditions, lodges, and abilities as fishermen and hunters.

Other members of the Corps of Discovery did not like the Clatsop Indians who lived near the fort. A sergeant compared them unfavorably to other Native Americans the party had met

When Meriwether Lewis and William Clark met Toussaint Charbonneau's wife Sacagawea, the Native American woman was six months pregnant. Her son Jean-Baptiste was born on February 11, 1805, and spent his infancy strapped to a cradleboard. We know this because with "Pomp" (as Clark nicknamed him) on her back, Sacagawea dove into the Missouri rapids to rescue Clark's journals. Without those, we would know much less about the Corps of Discovery's explorations and findings. Those journals also reveal Sacagawea's invaluable help and skill in negotiating, orienteering, and foraging. The leaders knew that the presence of a woman, especially one with a baby, would demonstrate their peaceful intentions to the Native Americans they encountered.

Sacagawea also acted as a translator. Lewis and Clark spoke English and some French; Charbonneau spoke French, English, and Shoshoni; Sacagawea spoke her native Shoshoni and Hidatsa (the language of the tribe that kidnapped her when she was 10). The Corps of Discovery needed to travel through Hidatsa territory in order to reach the Pacific coast. Without Sacagawea's ability to speak Hidatsa, the expedition would have had a very difficult time convincing that tribe to help them.

during their journey to the Pacific. "All the Indians from the Rocky Mountains to the falls of Columbia are an honest, ingenious and well disposed people; but from the falls to the seacoast, and along it, they are a rascally, thieving set."

Fort Clatsop was not the first fort in the West, and it certainly would not be last. It was, however, the first American fort at the edge of the nation's new **frontier**. Without its protection, the Corps of Discovery could not have weathered the winter to make their triumphant return, and no one would have learned of their scientific, **anthropological**, and **cartographic** discoveries.

The Continental Divide is like the spine of North America. It is the ridge of highest land running north and south through the Rocky Mountains. On the east side of the Continental Divide, the water that runs off the land will eventually make its way east and north; on the west side of the Divide runoff water will eventually reach the Pacific Ocean.

As is the case with many of the Spanish forts and missions in the West, the Presidio in San Francisco is still standing today. The view has changed considerably. When it was built, the area around the Presidio was uninhabited; now, the fort overlooks the dynamic city of San Francisco.

COLONIZATION: THE PRESIDIO OF SAN FRANCISCO

LEWIS AND CLARK WERE THE FIRST ANGLO-AMERICANS TO LEAD A PARTY TO THE NEW limits of the United States. They were not, however, the first Europeans to explore the North American continent's Pacific coast. Spanish explorers, who early in the 16th century had established the colony of New Spain in Mexico, were the first settlers in the American West. The Spanish established settlements in Texas, New Mexico, and Louisiana.

The reasons for Spain's interest in exploration and colonization are complicated. Like other countries that sent expeditions to the New World, part of their motivation was sheer curiosity. For the relatively small and populous countries of Europe, the idea of a large land filled with limitless natural resources was irresistible.

However, the **conquistadors** of Spain, including Hernán Cortés and Francisco Vasquez de Coronado (who first came to the West around 1540), were more than just curious. In an era of great expansion and wealth, they wanted to gain more land

Texas was part of Mexico for many years. After the Battle of San Jacinto in 1836, Texas became an independent republic. It did not become part of the United States until 1846. The 28th state is still known as "the Lone Star State" because of its period of independence.

and more wealth. Their government, a **monarchy**, supported this quest. So did the Roman Catholic Spanish church. The Church provided the conquistadors with a document called the *Requerimiento* that claimed to give the Spanish groups rights from God to conquer new territory and peoples.

The ties between Spain's church and state were also demonstrated by the work of monks who came to the New World in order to preach their faith and lifestyle to the Native Americans. Most early Spanish settlements were missions: fortifications constructed around a place of worship whose inhabitants swore loyalty to their crown in the name of God. One mission of this type was the *Presidio* of San Francisco.

Spain expanded to the Pacific territories in the second half of the 18th century, a time known as the Enlightenment. During the Enlightenment, many people were more interested in human beings' ability to reason and think than they were in the power of God. Religious missions became less popular.

However, California was far away from the other Spanish forts and outposts in the New World, and so the focus on God

☞ Father Junipero Serra was one of the many devoted Jesuit priests who came from Spain to convert the Native Californians to Christianity. Although the Spanish mission movement was started with good intentions, the men running the missions met a great deal of resistance from the Native Americans whose culture they perceived as sinful.

in Californian missions was less disturbed by the new thoughts of the Enlightenment. The Spanish missions did not experience the same kinds of activity that English and French forts of the same time period saw. The people of the missions kept to themselves, rather than interacting with the other nationalities in the area.

However, Spanish mission forts like the Presidio did interact with the Native American tribes. In much of what we now call California, the local tribes lived far apart from each

Mission San Francisco de Assisi, an early mission founded by Father Serra, was built in a much cruder style than some of the later mission complexes. When funds for the missions gradually increased, closer attention was paid to the quality and style of the buildings.

other and spoke very different dialects. The Spanish colonists found it easy to keep the tribes separated and to use the people as laborers for the missions. One of the first explorers of California, Sebastian Vizcaino, wrote from Monterey to King Carlos that the people were "gentle & affable" and would "receive readily … the holy gospel and will come into subjection to the royal crown."

The Presidio on San Francisco Bay was established in 1776 as the furthest outpost of the Spanish Empire in North America. Under the command of Jose Joaquin Moraga, a group of 30 soldiers and their families marched from Monterey to San Francisco and constructed a quadrangle with living quarters. Nearby, Father Junipero Serra built a mission he called San Francisco de Asis, later known as Mission Dolores.

Like Texas, California was its own country for a short time. Unlike Texas, which remained its own country for almost a decade, California's Bear Flag flew for just one month in 1846. California officially became the 29th state in 1850.

The original buildings that the Spanish settlers made of rough sticks and local stones were soon covered with adobe, a building material made from the clay in the soil. Unfortunately, although adobe was perfect for the dry season, when the rainy season came the clay would virtually melt off of the walls.

In 1792, the English sea captain George Vancouver was permitted a visit inside the Presidio and found "a square area … resembling a pound for cattle … one of its sides still uninclosed by the wall." The fourth wall of the original quadrangle was still incomplete 25 years after Moraga ordered construction to begin.

The Presidio's history was still incomplete, too. Spanish influence in the New World was decreasing as countries such as

England and France explored and colonized the East (England's 13 colonies), the North (Canada's eastern French provinces), and the South (New France in what is now Louisiana). By 1800, the Presidio was abandoned. Windblown sand covered the **magazine** and many of the buildings were roofless.

When Mexico gained its independence in 1822, California came under its domain. The Presidio changed allegiance, but its almost-ruined walls could not support much activity. When the United States fought a war with Mexico from 1846 to 1848, the U.S. military took over the Presidio with little resistance and maintained it first as a marine **garrison**. In 1848, California was transferred by treaty from Mexico to the United States. With the start of the Civil War, General Edwin Sumner took command of the Presidio. Under Sumner, the fort he called "the only spot about here suitable for a command of troops" was restored and completed. The Presidio has the distinction of being the only fort in North America over which the flags of three different countries have flown.

The United States continued to expand the Presidio, using it as a U.S. Army post until 1994. Cutbacks in the federal budget and a smaller military meant the old fort was then closed. The Presidio remains open to the public as part of the National Park Service's San Francisco Golden Gate National Recreation Area, which describes the fort's importance as follows: "As a U.S. Army post, the Presidio protected commerce and trade, and played a logistical role in every major U.S.

military conflict over the last 150 years. World events and those on the home front—from military campaigns to the rise of aviation, from World Fairs to natural disasters—left their mark here."

Spain did not keep control of California. However, Spain's construction of the Presidio ensured that Spanish influence is still felt in California.

👆 Posters like this one from 1879 advertised cheap land west of the Mississippi, available to pioneers to settle. The U.S. government and most of the settlers disregarded the feelings of the Native Americans already living on the land.

ENCAMPMENT: FORT LEAVENWORTH, KANSAS

HISTORIAN RICHARD WHITE HAS WRITTEN THAT THE "WEST COULD HAVE BEEN DIFFERENT." White means that people, circumstances, and events can sometimes form a crossroads. Take one road, and you end up placing a border at a river; take the other road, and you might place the same border along a mountain range. In 1827 the United States War Department told Colonel Henry Leavenworth to "take four companies of infantry, to ascend the Missouri River, and upon reaching a point within 20 miles of the mouth of the Little Platte River, to establish a **cantonment**."

The War Department believed a permanent fort was necessary in order to protect traders from increasingly hostile Native Americans on the Santa Fe Trail. Leavenworth's orders were to stay on the Missouri side of the river, but he found the land there flooded easily. The best spot, from the military perspective, was right across the river in Kansas territory. The cantonment Leavenworth established became the "gateway to the west," the first permanent settlement west of the Missouri River. It was also the first permanent American military post on the Western frontier.

From 1870 to 1916, soldiers from Fort Leavenworth were assigned as the guards for Yellowstone National Park.

Many historians have noted that the American "frontier" has changed many times in our nation's history. What does the word "frontier" mean? Generally speaking, it describes a place, region, or borderland that has not been officially claimed. A "frontier" opens up into territory that no one owns—yet.

Of course, today we understand that the American West as defined by its Missouri frontier had already been claimed. Its inhabitants, whom we now know as Native Americans, had occupied the land for centuries. But the U.S. government of the mid-19th century did not acknowledge the Native Americans' claim to their territory. The American government saw the western frontier as an area of unlimited possibility. So did the settlers heading west from Ohio, Georgia, and other American states.

For its first 30 years, Fort Leavenworth served mostly as the jumping-off point for those bound westward, a refueling and supply station for travelers. The soldiers stationed at the fort were responsible for protecting settlers while they made their way to new homesteads and traded with the Native Americans.

During the late 18th century, while the country still saw the western territories as nearly boundless, the U.S. government drew up the ordinances of 1785 and 1787 to divide those territories. The system of grids imposed didn't always make much sense; one "square" would contain flat farmland, while another would contain rocky and mountainous terrain. But the government believed that this system would make it easy and fair for people to purchase land lots.

Emigrants from the East were moving in broad streams across the mountains and spilling over into the nearest regions that would contain them. It was only a matter of time

Many settlers thought nothing of driving wagon trains through lands that were sacred to the Native Americans. The Indians often protested the passage of settlers' wagons, as in this 1874 drawing.

Fort Leavenworth, Kansas, was a safe haven for travelers across the unfamiliar territory of America's Midwest. Many settlers passed through Fort Leavenworth because it was so close to the Missouri River. Rather than traveling overland, settlers could reach the beginning of the Oregon Trail by riverboat. This photograph of the barracks at Fort Leavenworth was taken during the late 19th century.

before those broad streams of people reached across the Missouri River into new places that were not yet divided and did not yet have borders.

The Old West consisted of the Piedmont and the Appalachian Valleys. It attracted all sorts of settlers. Often those settlers were people fleeing poverty and hardship or trouble and the law. Each time settlers formed a new frontier, tension developed between them and the government back in the East. Although government regulations prohibited settlement of many Indian lands at this time, dissatisfied settlers were constantly pushing at the borders, trying to go further into the "New West."

Many settlers passed through Fort Leavenworth because it was so close to the Missouri River. Rather than traveling overland, settlers could reach the beginning of the Oregon Trail by riverboat.

Fur traders and mountain men brought back tales from the Pacific of fertile valleys and rolling plains. After 1835, many people began to follow the Oregon Trail in hopes of finding those places themselves. The trail began at Independence, Missouri, and wound westward for about 2,000 miles (3,200 kilometers) across the Great Plains and the Rocky Mountains to the rich valleys of the Oregon region. Pioneer farmers, cattle ranchers, and sheep ranchers journeyed westward along the trail. Fort Leavenworth, just across the river from Independence, acted as a sort of funnel for all the traffic to the New West.

The soldiers had many roles to play, and they needed to have facilities available to them that would allow them to do their jobs. An early frontier fort had separate quarters for the officers and enlisted men, an enclosed area for drill, and rooms to store weapons: the **battery**, the powder magazine, and the gun shed. Depending upon the number of soldiers, a frontier fort might have a chapel, a schoolhouse for family members, and some shops. For example, in 1824, Fort Snelling, Minnesota, had a bakeshop, as well as blacksmith, carpenter, armorer, wheelwright, and harness shops. Fort Leavenworth had these and also had a "sutler's store," later known as the

Members of the U.S. Ninth Cavalry are on the trail in this painting by Don Stivers. The African-American troopers, nicknamed Buffalo Soldiers, established an admirable record during numerous campaigns in the 1870s and 1880s. The Buffalo Soldiers were stationed at Fort Leavenworth, Kansas.

post exchange, where a military shopkeeper sold manufactured goods.

Fort Leavenworth saw many different types of activity. In 1839, Colonel S. W. Kearny marched against the Cherokees with the largest U.S. mounted force yet assembled: 10 companies of **dragoons**. In 1846 Colonel A. W. Doniphan set out on his Mexican expedition, and throughout the war with Mexico the fort was the outfitting post for the army of the West. During the 1850s, wagon teams hauled supplies over the Santa Fe Trail, the Oregon Trail, and other routes to all forts, posts, and military camps of the West, some as far away as the Pacific. Fort Leavenworth boasted huge supply yards and corrals that allowed it to receive and protect large amounts of goods.

When Kansas Territory was organized in 1854, Governor Andrew Reeder set up executive offices at Fort Leavenworth. After the Civil War, Leavenworth became home to the first permanent all-black regiments in the U.S. Army, known as the Buffalo Soldiers. In 1874, the first military prison was established there, a self-supporting operation where the prisoners quarried rock and built homes for the post. In 1881, General William T. Sherman established the school that later became the Command and General Staff College, the highest tactical school in the Army educational system. A 1926 graduate, with highest honors in his class, was Major Dwight D. Eisenhower.

Groups of settlers traveled together in wagon trains to make the long, tedious, and dangerous trek along the Oregon Trail to their lands in the west.

EXPANSION: FORT LARAMIE, WYOMING

California, depending on the route taken once a traveler reached Fort Bridger in Wyoming. In 1843, when the first "Great Migration" to the West occurred, California was part of Mexico, Oregon was part of England, and most of the land between those places and Missouri was considered a "region of savages and wild beasts," in the words of statesman Daniel Webster.

No matter how risky it seemed to for a family to sell their land, pick up their possessions, and begin a 2,000-mile trek, people were willing to go. So many went that the journey was less lonely and dangerous than we might think.

The chief case of death on the trail was not animal attack or Indian ambush but cholera. Cholera was a highly contagious disease that could be spread even from wagon wheels to humans. The more traffic on the trail, the more cholera spread.

When Fort Laramie was closed in 1890, the last soldiers were marched out before the buildings and equipment were sold at auction.

But the men, women, and children who set forth on the Oregon Trail were determined and often had strong reasons behind their actions. From the economic panic of 1837–42 to the Gold Rush Fever of 1849–50, people were once again seeing new lands with new eyes. They were hoping to have their part in the bounty of the West.

There were other events that hastened westward migration as well. For example, as more and more settlers reached the farm-friendly fields of Oregon, their homesteads forced Great Britain to negotiate the boundary between the United States and Canada. The Oregon Treaty of 1846 gave the Columbia River Valley to the United States once and for all.

While the first part of the trail was geographically quite easygoing, it was still a difficult journey. Francis Parkman, an historian who made the trip West himself in 1836, illustrated just how long and stressful it was when he wrote: "We have passed the more tedious part of the journey; but four hundred miles still intervened between us and Fort Laramie; and to reach that point cost us the travel of three more weeks…Before and behind us the level monotony of the plain was unbroken as far as the eye could reach."

Most people traveled in groups of the familiar covered

Fort Laramie in Wyoming was accessible to traders, soldiers, and Native Americans. Located along the Oregon Trail, the structure also provided a safe haven for weary travelers. This painting of the fort was made around 1845 by W. H. Jackson, who would become a famous painter and photographer of the American West.

wagons, known as "Prairie Schooners," pulled by slow but dependable oxen. One of the first and most welcome stops for these travelers on the trail was a fortification just north of the Laramie and North Platte Rivers in eastern Wyoming. Fort Laramie, originally known as Fort William, had been constructed as a fur trading post. It was eventually sold to John Jacob Astor's American Fur Company and renamed Fort John. In 1849, the fort was sold to the U.S. Army. Fort John-on-the-Laramie became known simply as Fort Laramie, and was never used as a real military post. Its main purpose was to provide some degree of protection to emigrants heading west on the trail. Fort Laramie's soldiers were there only to keep it open and functioning, rather than to conduct campaigns or to protect their garrison.

Like Fort Leavenworth, Fort Laramie had a post "sutler" who ran a combination general store, post office, and supply house. (The Fort Laramie post office, established in 1850, is the oldest continuously operating post office in Wyoming.) The Sutler Store was probably the most important part of Fort Laramie for travelers who arrived there low on food and other supplies, fatigued from riding in their canvas-covered wagons. Often families had to leave precious belongings on the trail because the weight of the wagons was too much for the working animals. Even if they could not replace furniture or china, the Sutler Store was a welcome reminder of civilization.

And travelers arrived at Fort Laramie constantly. From the 1,000 settlers in the Great Migration brought through by Marcus and Narcissa Whitman to the first Mormon emigrants, Fort Laramie saw most of the major pioneer groups pass through its area. Famous explorers like Kit Carson and John Frémont, military leaders like General William S. Harney and General Philip Sheridan, Native American chiefs Crazy Horse and Red Cloud, and "Wild West" personalities like Wyatt Earp and Calamity Jane all came through Fort Laramie. Over 100,000 emigrants passed through Fort Laramie between 1849 and 1890

It took at least four months for emigrating settlers to get to Oregon, and one of the worst problems was not disease or danger, but boredom. Births, marriages, and other celebrations in camps helped to relieve the monotonous trip.

The men and their families posted at Fort Laramie must have welcomed the new faces. Life on a Western fort could be unbearably dull, consisting mostly of scheduled daily drills and chores. Chores included building roads, carrying water, chopping wood, and caring for horses and other animals. No matter where a fort was located, in all seasons men wore woolen trousers and jackets with flannel shirts.

Army wives who lived on posts like Fort Laramie had to endure most of the same problems as their husbands, without the distraction of military drills or field action. Food was not as scarce on the fort as it was on the trail, but it was bland and hardly varied: salt pork, hardtack (crackers), beans, and coffee, with occasional fresh vegetables. The women wore sunbonnets and plain dresses made of cotton **calico** and **gingham**.

Besides travelers famous and nonfamous, Western forts did offer some amusements. The men played cards, gambled, drank, and tossed horseshoes, while the women held

The life of John Charles Frémont (1813–1890) reads like an adventure novel. His mother was a Southern belle who ran away with a Frenchman and gave birth to an illegitimate child. Without connections or money, the young John Frémont set out to make his way in the world. He managed to get a job with the Army Corps of Topographical Engineers and helped to survey the southern Appalachian Mountains and later the upper Mississippi and Missouri Rivers.

Frémont's reputation attracted the attention of powerful Missouri senator Thomas Hart Benton. The young soldier then attracted the eye of Benton's talented daughter Jessie, and they eloped in 1841. Jessie Benton Frémont cultivated Frémont's reputation as "the Pathfinder," editing his reports, which were published in all of the nation's newspapers.

Frémont mapped the path to the Columbia River with Christopher "Kit" Carson, was briefly the civil governor of California, ran unsuccessfully for president in 1856, won promotion to major general during the Civil War, and made and lost over $10 million in the California Gold Rush.

quilting bees and canning parties. Most settlements, including forts, had small lending libraries. Sundays were reserved for relaxation and church attendance, although sometimes worship didn't resemble its Eastern counterpart. Children helped with chores and learned to ride horses when they weren't attending makeshift schools. (The first school in the state of Wyoming was established at Fort Laramie in 1856, with the post chaplain, Reverend Vaux, acting as schoolmaster.)

One of the most notable aspects of frontier fort life was the presence of Native Americans. Settlers feared the "savages" while traveling the Trail, but once at a post, most white folk would happily trade with them. At Fort Laramie, Native Americans provided the men of the fort with wild horses, buffalo meat, and hides. While soldiers posted to frontier forts were supposed to limit the amount of alcohol they allowed Native Americans to obtain, in reality the soldiers regularly offered liquor as trade.

Between 1851 and 1854, Fort Laramie saw its longest peace between whites and Indians. However, the tide was about to turn.

INDIANS. FORT SILL.

👆 Comanche tribal leaders stand on the grounds of Fort Sill, Oklahoma, in 1895. The site was used as a U.S. field artillery center.

5

EXPULSION: FORT SILL, OKLAHOMA

ANGLO-AMERICANS AND OTHERS HEADING
WEST WERE NOT THE ONLY PEOPLE TO PASS BY
Fort Laramie. In September 1851, the largest gathering of
native tribes was held at Horse Creek, 35 miles from the
Wyoming outpost. The meeting was attended by 10,000
Native Americans, tribes ranging from the Teton Sioux to the
Arikara to the Shoshoni, camping in tipis in this valley on the
Oregon Trail.

While this was the largest gathering of Indians ever to be
seen on the Plains, the tribes had not organized the meeting.
The U.S. government had called them together because federal
officials realized that the "permanent Indian frontier"
established years earlier would not work. Although the Indians
had been promised that land beyond the Mississippi would be
theirs, the Westward Movement, the California Gold Rush, and
other expansion opportunities had affected their boundary.

As more and more white settlers pushed into Indian
territory, government and military leaders feared the Indians
would seek **retribution**. The 1851 Horse Creek Gathering was

One of the most famous speeches made by a Native American chief is known as "How Can You Buy the Sky," made by Chief Seattle of the Suquamish tribe in 1854. Environmentalists seeking to show the impossibility of owning the land often quote it.

an attempt to appease the Indians. Colonel Thomas Fitzpatrick told the gathered tribes that the "Great Father"—the U.S. government— would compensate the Indians for their losses in land, hunting, and natural resources. Of course, the government wanted something in return. It would pay the tribes $50,000 per year if they would confine themselves to specific areas and keep off of the trails west used by settlers. Although no one was yet using the word "reservation," this was the beginning of the reservation system.

This treaty and others that followed were doomed to failure because neither side fully realized what was being asked of the Native Americans. The U.S. government did not understand how vital space and freedom were to the tribes' way of life. Native Americans did not understand that their chiefs' signatures on pieces of paper took their space and freedom away forever.

Just three years later, troops from Fort Laramie under the command of Second Lieutenant John Grattan would interfere in a Miniconju Sioux tribesman's dispute over a settler's butchered cow. Hundreds of Lakota Sioux butchered Grattan's

☛ Red Cloud was a Sioux chief who was angry with settlers entering his territory in Montana. Between 1866 and 1868 he led a successful war against the United States. Red Cloud's War ended with the 1868 Treaty of Fort Laramie.

men, and peace on the Western plains was broken.

Many **skirmishes** would follow the "Grattan Massacre," including the Long Walk of the Apache herded to a reservation in New Mexico, the Great Sioux Uprising, and the Sand Creek Massacre of 1862. The Civil War (1861–1865) lessened conflicts with the Indians because the U.S. government had to focus its energies and resources on other military matters.

In June 1866, however, Native Americans and U.S. officials once more gathered at Fort Laramie. The Fort Laramie Council began negotiations similar to the earlier Horse Creek Gathering.

General William T. Sherman meets with Sioux, Cheyenne, and Arapaho chiefs at Fort Laramie in 1868. The treaty ended Red Cloud's War and promised the Sioux the Black Hills of South Dakota and the Powder River Valley as hunting grounds. Unfortunately, the United States violated the treaty almost immediately.

The U.S. offered money—this time $75,000—to the Indians in exchange for peace and safe passage for settlers on the Bozeman Trail. However, a young Oglala Sioux chief known as Red Cloud was furious when he learned of U.S. plans to build new forts in the heart of Teton Sioux territory. He cried, "The Great White Father sends us presents and wants us to sell him the road, but the White chief goes with soldiers to steal the road before the Indians can say yes or no! I will talk with you no more!"

Only days later, Red Cloud's warriors were attacking groups of soldiers and wreaking havoc in Montana territory. Commanders desperately issued regulations to keep troops posted at Western forts safe from ambush, sniping, and scalping. On September 21, 1866, Colonel Henry Carrington

Many people know General George Custer's name, but his brother Tom Custer, a captain in the army, was also a war hero who won the Congressional Medal of Honor. Tom Custer died alongside his older brother at the battle of Little Bighorn in 1876.

issued new security measures, including orders such as this one: "Upon a general alarm or appearance of Indians in force or near the gates, the same will be closed, and no soldier or civilian will leave the fort without orders... All horses of mounted men will be saddled at reveille"

After two years of fighting, U.S. government leaders met with Red Cloud at Fort Laramie. The government agreed to close three forts and keep white settlers out of the Sioux's sacred lands, the Black Hills. In return, Red Cloud ended the fighting. However, Americans soon broke the treaty, and relations between the whites and Native Americans continued to be hostile.

The hostility wasn't new; it had existed for a long time in

When Mr. Stanford L. Davis, a California schoolteacher, retired and began to research his genealogy, he discovered that his great-grandfather Henry Parker had been one of the African American "Buffalo Soldiers."

Henry Parker was born a slave in Kentucky, but escaped in 1864, joined the Army as a private in the 101st Regiment United States Colored Infantry, and served in the Civil War. Afterward, he re-enlisted for five years in 1867 with Company D of the 10th U.S. Cavalry, a unit of the Buffalo Soldiers.

Under the command of Colonel Benjamin Grierson, the 10th Cavalry was one of the first units to camp at Medicine Bluff, which would become Fort Sill, Oklahoma. Parker served until his 1877 discharge at Fort Concho, Texas, with the rank of sergeant, a place on the Color Guard, and an "excellent" character. Stan Davis has created a Web site with his research on his great-grandfather, history of the Buffalo Soldiers, and more: www.buffalosoldiers.net

Check it out—you may be inspired to look into your own history!

different places and to different degrees. What was new was the extent of government interference. As the U.S. government appointed more and more public servants to oversee Indian affairs, and built more and more fortifications to protect U.S. interests, the hostility changed from hatred between civilizations to hatred between oppressor and oppressed.

One of the key players in this clash of civilizations was Major General Philip H. Sheridan, a Civil War hero and a brash commander with little regard for the Native American

🦬 General Philip Sheridan, who had been a successful leader during the Civil War, named Fort Sill after a friend killed in the war. Sheridan went on to be one of the most formidable opponents of Native Americans, who were being forced off of their land.

people or their lifestyles. In 1869, Sheridan led six **cavalry** regiments into Indian Territory, now Oklahoma. The campaign was supposed to stop hostile Indian tribes from raiding settlements on the border of Kansas. Because it was January, the troops needed to be housed, and the first hastily constructed garrison was called "Camp Wichita."

Shortly after that, Sheridan christened the new post Fort Sill, Oklahoma, in honor of Brigadier General Joshua W. Sill, who had been killed in the Civil War. Sill had been a friend and classmate of Sheridan at the U.S. Military Academy. The new post was home

One of the most famous residents of Fort Sill was Geronimo, the Apache chief who battled American soldiers and settlers in the southwest during the 1870s and 1880s. Geronimo died in 1909 and was buried at the fort.

to the six regiments brought west by Sheridan, including the 7th Cavalry, the 19th Kansas Volunteers, and the 10th Cavalry. The 10th Cavalry was a group of African American soldiers who were known as the "Buffalo Soldiers." Although the 10th Cavalry was a distinguished group who had shown much courage in battle, they were not given many military responsibilities. Instead, they were placed in charge of construction. They built many of the stone buildings on the post quadrangle.

Fort Sill had a mission to protect Native Americans remaining on the south plains until the territory taken by the U.S. government opened for settlement. In 1875 Quanah Parker and his Quohada Comanches arrived at Fort Sill, the last of the active Indian warriors. In 1894 a group of 342 Apache prisoners of war were brought to the Oklahoma post. The most famous man in that group was Geronimo, the last Indian leader to formally surrender to the U.S. government. Until his surrender in 1886, Geronimo's **guerilla** warfare had terrified many settlers in New Mexico and Arizona. By 1894, however, he was a defeated man. He traveled for a while with Pawnee Bill's Wild West Show and died in 1909 of pneumonia. His Fort Sill gravesite is located, ironically, on Quanah Road.

Chief Geronimo's Band of Apache, as they became known, remained on at Fort Sill until 1913. Some of them joined Troop L of the 7th Cavalry, an Indian unit that helped avert a South Plains version of the Ghost Dance Uprising in 1897. Their commander, Lieutenant Hugh L. Scott, taught them to build houses, raise crops, and herd cattle. They needed these skills after the last Indian lands opened to settlers in 1901. The Western frontier had virtually disappeared.

👆 Fort Hood stretches into the distance. Life in a modern fort of the West is much safer and easier than it was during the late 19th century.

MODERNIZATION: FORT HOOD, TEXAS

TODAY FORT SILL, THE U.S. ARMY FIELD ARTILLERY CENTER, IS A BUSY MILITARY POST next to the town of Lawton, Oklahoma. It is the only active army installation on the South Plains that was built during the Indian Wars. There are other Army posts in other parts of the West, including the Presidio and Fort Leavenworth, that have historic connections to the American frontier, of course.

In modern times, after the Old West disappeared, many Western forts have also been built. While some of these forts are temporary, many others are permanent posts designed for modern military needs. The first major war of the 20th century, World War I, took place in Europe, closest to the East Coast and its fortifications. But World War II began for the United States at Pearl Harbor, Hawaii, in the Pacific. The West was closer to this war both geographically and mentally. Western states had large areas of undeveloped land that could be used for training troops, testing weapons, and storing equipment.

One of the first sites selected in 1941 for a new military post was located in the middle of Texas. Camp Hood opened

General John Bell Hood, for whom Camp Hood was named, only commanded his Texas Brigade for six months in 1862, but his leadership was so daring and remarkable that his name remained on the unit for the rest of the Civil War.

in 1942 and was named for a Confederate general named John Bell Hood. He had been a noted cavalryman and commander of Hood's Texas Brigade. Camp Hood, run by the Air Force, became Fort Hood in 1951. In 1952 Fort Hood became an Army post, and it remains one today.

Fort Hood is called "the Army's premier installation to train and deploy heavy forces." In fulfilling that role, it has grown to be the world's single largest military installation. North of Austin, the Texas state capital, and south of Dallas, Fort Hood covers 340 square miles or 217,337 acres of land. The weather is dry and the temperature stable for much of the year; combined with mostly flat terrain, these conditions are ideal for military maneuvers like road marches and artillery practice. Fort Hood has two large mechanized divisions: the First Cavalry Division and the Fourth Infantry Division, both of which fall under its largest and most diverse unit—Headquarters, III Corps. Nearly 50,000 soldiers are assigned to Fort Hood, although some units are deployed or located elsewhere.

Many soldiers stationed there are young and unmarried. The average age of a soldier at Fort Hood is 20. There are barracks

🖐 General John Bell Hood was Fort Hood's namesake. His bravery and strong leadership for the Confederate side during the Civil War inspired his men and earned him recognition and respect.

for single soldiers on post at Fort Hood. At training areas, barracks can take the form of long, low buildings with rows of simple iron bedsteads. For soldiers permanently assigned to Fort Hood (usually for a period of two to four years), barracks rooms are constructed for two people with a shared bathroom

During the 19th century, most of the forts of the West were established as solitary outposts on the American frontier. Over the years many of the small settlements around these forts have grown up into cities.

or "latrine." Modern soldiers are allowed to have many of the items college students of the same age would have in their rooms: stereos, mini-refrigerators, telephones, and televisions. However, soldiers have to be ready to have their rooms inspected at any time by their superior officers.

Like their counterparts in earlier Western forts, modern soldiers have strict schedules. A soldier at Fort Lincoln in 1868 might have awakened at 5:30 A.M. when trumpets sounded reveille. He would have then gone immediately to the stable to groom and feed the horses. His day would have ended at about 9:30 P.M. after several drills. A soldier at Fort Hood today usually awakens at about 5:30 for physical training, or "PT." After an hour of running and exercises (push-ups and sit-ups are most important), the soldier will shower and have breakfast before reporting for duty. The different jobs soldiers hold at Fort Hood are as varied as the post is large: some soldiers

Fort Hood is now the site of the Comanche National Indian Cemetery, built in 1991 on an archaeological site where scientists found remains of an older Native American burial ground.

train for combat in the infantry or armor (modern cavalry), some soldiers take care of equipment in large motor pools, and others help plan maneuvers. Still others perform administrative tasks, cook in the mess halls, and work as orderlies and medics at the hospital.

Along with soldiers often come families: wives, husbands, children, and sometimes even extended family members like grandparents. Fort Hood offers support services for nearly 75,000 family members. Married soldiers can often choose to live in houses on post built by the government. Family members can shop at the post exchange (remember the sutler's store?), buy groceries at the **commissary**, and make appointments with military doctors and dentists. Fort Hood has five different elementary schools for the children of soldiers who live on post and many different youth centers, playgrounds, and gymnasium facilities. Like many modern Army

Dr. Samuel Billison, Native American educator, might seem an unlikely candidate for a G.I. Joe doll. But one of the action figures is not only modeled after him—it contains his voice. Billison, who recorded the lines for "Navajo Code Talker G.I. Joe," was one of the original 29 Navajo recruited to construct the only unbroken military code in history.

Billison was also one of the six Navajo Code Talkers at Iwo Jima during World War II. Their job was to broadcast messages between groups of American soldiers that could not be understood by the Japanese defending Iwo Jima. The Code Talkers fashioned a new "dialect" of their language, which has no alphabet or symbols. Since only about 30 non-Navajo could speak the language when the war began, it was a self-contained, unbreakable communication system. Dr. Billison's lightning-fast transmissions of over 800 error-free commands led an officer to declare: "Were it not for the Navajos, the Marines would never have taken Iwo Jima."

Samuel Billison, who is president of the Navajo Code Talkers Association, says, "Native American language is very powerful and very sacred." August 14 was proclaimed by President Ronald Reagan in 1982 as Navajo Code Talkers Day.

posts, Fort Hood resembles a small city with cars, bicycles, and motorcycles; children at school and at play; houses, stores, and office buildings; a library, a post office, and chapels. There is even a movie theater and a fast-food restaurant!

Unlike earlier fortifications, Fort Hood is not walled in, nor are there specific barriers at every point. For the present time, the main entrances are marked and have guardhouses.

Sometimes military police, or "MPs," stop motorists and pedestrians to check identification cards. Every adult, whether an active-duty soldier, a family member, or a government employee, must carry a Department of Defense identification card.

While attacks from hostile tribes or wild animals are no longer a worry for modern armed forces, the government needs to be sure that no one tries to misuse the forts.

Like earlier fortifications, Fort Hood has influenced its surroundings. The city of Killeen, Texas, has grown up around and with the fort. Other area towns, including Copperas Cove to the west and Harker Heights to the east, provide housing choices for the many soldiers and their families who do not live on post. The towns were at first dependent on the inhabitants of the fort for business, but as their populations have increased, these towns have become more self-sufficient.

Fort Hood may not seem as interesting or glamorous as its predecessors, but "the Great Place" (as the Army calls it) carries on the old tradition of providing services to travelers (in this case, military people) and establishing a government presence in a particular area.

GLOSSARY

Anthropological

Having to do with the study of human beings.

Battery

A group of artillery weapons.

Calico

An inexpensive cotton fabric, usually printed with flowers or other small shapes.

Cantonment

Temporary quarters for troops.

Cartographic

Having to do with the making of maps.

Cavalry

Mounted troops.

Commissary

A store for equipment and provisions.

Conquistadors

The Spanish conquerors of the New World.

Dragoons

Heavily armed mounted troops.

Emigrants

People who leave their home to move to another land or region.

Frontier

The region on the edge of civilized and settled land.

Garrison

A military post.

Gingham

A plain fabric made from yarn-dyed cotton.

Guerilla

A form of fighting that makes use of sabotage and harassment.

Magazine

A place where explosives and other ammunition are stored.

Monarchy

The form of government where a king or queen has absolute power to rule.

Retribution

Punishment or revenge.

Skirmishes

Small battles.

Smokehouse

A building where meat or fish is preserved with dense smoke.

TIMELINE

1540

Spanish conquistadors come to the New World.

1776

The Presidio is built on San Francisco Bay in California by the Spanish.

1805

Lewis and Clark build Fort Clatsop in Oregon territory.

1822

Mexico wins its independence from Spain, and the Presidio becomes a Mexican fort.

1827

Fort Leavenworth is built.

1846

Oregon becomes a U.S. territory.

1848

California becomes part of the United States, and the Presidio becomes an American fort.

1849

California Gold Rush begins; Fort Laramie becomes a U.S. fort.

1851

The Horse Creek Gathering of Native Americans takes place near Fort Laramie.

1861–1865

The American Civil War.

1869

Fort Sill is built in Oklahoma as a base for the military aggression against Native Americans.

1874

Fort Leavenworth becomes a military prison.

1881

The Command and General Staff College is established at Fort Leavenworth.

1886

Geronimo is brought to Fort Sill.

1890

Fort Laramie is closed.

1942

Camp Hood opens in Texas.

1994

The Presidio is closed as an active military fort.

FURTHER READING

Ambrose, Stephen E. *Undaunted Courage: Meriweather Lewis, Thomas Jefferson, and the Opening of the American West*. New York: Touchstone, 1997.

Binns, Tristan Boyer. *Fort Laramie*. Portsmouth, N.H.: Heinemann, 2001.

Copeland, Peter F. *Historic North American Forts*. New York: Dover, 2000.

De Voto, Beranard Augustine. *Across the Wide Missouri*. New York: Houghton Mifflin, 1998.

Hedren, Paul Lo. *Fort Laramie and the Great Sioux War*. Norman: University of Oklahoma Press, 1998.

Hine, Robert V. and John Mack Faragher. *The American West: A New Interpretive History*. New Haven, Conn.: Yale University Press, 2000.

Legg, John. *Treaty at Fort Laramie*. New York: St. Martin's, 1994.

Mattes, Merrill J. *The Great Platte River Road: The Covered Wagon Mainline Via Fort Keary to Fort Laramie*. Lincoln: University of Nebraska, 1987.

Maynard, Charles W. *Fort Laramie*. New York: Powerkids, 2001.

Nadeau, Remi A. *Fort Laramie and the Sioux*. New York: Crest, 1997.

Roberts, David. *A Newer World: Kit Carson, John C. Frémont, and the Claiming of the American West*. New York: Simon and Schuster, 2000.

Webber, Bert and Margie Webber. *Fort Laramie: Outpost on the Plains*. New York: Webb, 1999.

INTERNET RESOURCES

Famous Pioneers, Towns, Forts, & Places

http://www.americanwest.com

Western Trails, Mountain Passes, Forts

http://www.linecamp.com/museums/americanwest/hubs/trails_mountain_
  passes_forts/trails_mountain_passes_forts.html

Forts and Historical Sites

http://www.homepages.dsu.edu/Jankej/oldwest/forts.htm

http://www.coax.net

http://www2.h-net.msu.edu/~west/archives/logsjun95/0015.html

http://www.americanwest.com

http://www.linecamp.com/museums/americanwest/hubs/trails_mountain_
  passes_forts/trails_mountain_passes_forts.html

Fort Clatsop

http://www.nps.gov/focl/

http://us.f148.mail.yahoo.com/ym/login?.rand=2eik651erehl7

Fort Laramie

http://www.nps.gov/fola/

http://www.fortlaramie.com/

http://www.yale.edu/lawweb/avalon/ntreaty/ntreaty.htm

http://grounder.freeyellow.com/ftlaramie.html

The Presidio

http://www.nps.gov/goga/

http://us.f148.mail.yahoo.com/ym/login?.rand=2eik651erehl7

Fort Sill

http://sill-www.army.mil/

Fort Hood

http://us.f148.mail.yahoo.com/ym/login?.rand=2eik651erehl7

INDEX

Black Hills, 45
Bozeman Trail, 44
Buffalo Soldiers, 48

Calamity Jane, 36
California, 16-21
Carrington, Henry, 45
Carson, Kit, 35
Charbonneau, Toussaint le, 8
Cherokee Indians, 29
Civil War, 20, 29, 43, 47
Clark, William Rogers, 7, 9-11, 15
Clatsop Indians, 12
Continental Divide, 7
Coronado, Francisco Vasquez de, 15
Corps of Discovery, 7-8, 11-13
Cortés, Hernán, 15
Crazy Horse, 36

Doniphan, A.W., 29
Drouillard, Georges, 8

Earp, Wyatt, 36
Eisenhower, Dwight D., 29
Enlightenment, 16-17

Fitzpatrick, Thomas, 42
Forts of the West
  Fort Clatsop, 8-13
  Fort Hood, 51-57
  Fort Laramie, 33-39, 41-45
  Fort Leavenworth, 23-29, 35, 51
  Fort Lincoln, 54-55
  Fort Sill, 47-49, 51
  Fort Snelling, 28
  Presidio, 16-21, 51
  San Francisco de Asis (Mission
  Delores), 19

Frémont, John, 35

Geronimo, 49
Ghost Dance Uprising, 49
Gold Rush, 32, 41
Grattan, John, 42-43
Great Plains, 27
Great Sioux Uprising, 43

Harney, William S., 35
Hood, John Bell, 52
Horse Creek Gathering, 41-42, 43

Jefferson, Thomas, 7

Kearney, S.W., 29

Leavenworth, Henry, 23
Lewis, Meriwether, 7, 9-11, 15
Long Walk of the Apache, 43
Louisiana Purchase, 7

Mexico, 15, 20, 29
Missouri River, 7, 23, 26
Moraga, Jose Joaquin, 19

Native Americans, 10-13, 17, 23, 24,
  41-49

Oregon Trail, 27, 29, 31, 32, 41

Pacific Northwest, 8
Pacific Ocean, 7, 15, 29, 51
Parker, Quanah, 49

Red Cloud, 36, 44-45
Reeder, Andrew, 29
Rocky Mountains, 13, 27

Sacagawea, 8
Sand Creek Massacre, 43
Santa Fe Trail, 23, 29
Scott, Hugh L., 49
Serra, Junipero, 19
Sheridan, Philip, 36, 46–48
Sherman, William T., 29
Sill, Joshua W., 47
Spain, 15, 16
Sumner, Edwin, 20

U.S. Army, 8, 20, 29, 34

Vancouver, George, 19
Vizcaino, Sebastian, 18

Webster, Daniel, 31
White, Richard, 23
Whitman, Marcus, 35
Whitman, Narcissa, 35
World War I, 51
World War II, 51

PHOTO CREDITS

AUTHOR

Bethanne Kelly Patrick is a freelance writer and curriculum specialist in English composition. One of the original writers for the Core Knowledge Series, she has authored a middle-school workbook on writing from literature. She is the "Military Legends" columnist for Military.com and is at work on a family travel guide to the Southwest, where she lives with her husband and two daughters.